The Spirit of Business

By
Phoenix Jackson

Published by Motivational Press, Inc.
1777 Aurora Road
Melbourne, Florida, 32935
www.MotivationalPress.com

Copyright 2018 © by Kelley Phoenix Jackson

All Rights Reserved

No part of this book may be reproduced or transmitted in any form by any means: graphic, electronic, or mechanical, including photocopying, recording, taping or by any information storage or retrieval system without permission, in writing, from the authors, except for the inclusion of brief quotations in a review, article, book, or academic paper. The authors and publisher of this book and the associated materials have used their best efforts in preparing this material. The authors and publisher make no representations or warranties with respect to accuracy, applicability, fitness or completeness of the contents of this material. They disclaim any warranties expressed or implied, merchantability, or fitness for any particular purpose. The authors and publisher shall in no event be held liable for any loss or other damages, including but not limited to special, incidental, consequential, or other damages. If you have any questions or concerns, the advice of a competent professional should be sought.

Manufactured in the United States of America.

ISBN: 978-1-62865-528-5

Contents

Dedication & Acknowledgements 5
Introduction 7

SECTION 1 11
So, you want to start a business?

Chapter 1 12
   Purpose
Chapter 2 16
   Acceptance. Commitment. Optimism.
Chapter 3 18
   Intuition

SECTION 2 25
Digging In

Chapter 4 26
   The Spirit of Business
Chapter 5 31
   Intuition II
Chapter 6 33
   The Doubt Monster

SECTION 3 47
Figuring It Out

Chapter 7 48
   Intention

Chapter 8 57
    What Not To Do
Chapter 9 59
    Movement Within Awareness
Chapter 10 64
    Commitment
Chapter 11 68
    Activating Discipline

SECTION 4 73
    Get to Business

Chapter 12 74
    Distraction. Catalyst. Deterrent.
Chapter 13 89
    Strength
Chapter 14 93
    Strategic Planning
Chapter 15 100
    Begin Creating

Dedication & Acknowledgements

I would like to dedicate this book The Spirit of Business to my son Simba Ausar. His light protects, radiates, and co-creates with me daily. I am grateful that he came through me, for the world. Namaste Young Master. I love you Ausar.

I would like to acknowledge my tribe whom have been in my life for many years and who have been a part of aligning, adjusting and allowing me to shine with support and love. I love you Nana Marilyn and Baba Theo. Your elder wisdom has been invaluable as it has held me up in times of darkness. I thank you for being my Light Bearers through the years. Dad, I appreciate your willingness to always share a fresh perspective on things. Oddly you make me think differently about things all the time. I appreciate the journey we have had as father and daughter. You are one of the most generous spirits that I know. I love you. Mom, your indomitable spirit is like none other and you taught me determination and strength. I have enjoyed watching you evolve in this life together. I love you. To all 7 of my siblings, I love you and want the best for you. I want you to heal, to grow and to become the highest versions of yourself.

Thank you to my friends who have been an intricate part of my evolution. I love you Ellie Zo (thank you for the years of listening, uplifting me and loving me when I was burning amidst the fire). Phoenix II, your wisdom flows like no other, 20 years is a long time to love someone and we have many more to go! I love you Ashton, Jennifer, Christy, Dafna, Sally, Shay, and Ashley. Your presence in my life is so unique and our creations together are ever evolving.

As not to leave anyone out, to many of my other friends, associates and extended family, I am thankful for your words of encouragement and unwavering support as you push me to keep going forward. Our conversations and our time was necessary and needed. I honor you.

A special thank you and shout out of love to family member D. Jeffrey who was the first to read the early chapters in this book. Your enthusiasm and feedback kept me focused and excited about moving forward. Your response inspired me.

Thank you, Alexa and Derrick Martin, your support and love as we have manifested our dreams collectively and alongside each other, has been a deep and true blessing. Derrick you have always seen and helped create the vision and Alexa you have in many ways supported it. Thank you for editing this book. I love you two! Well... you six!

Thank you to my many clients and business associates through the years who have been a part of building my expertise and character. Thank you to my students at the University of Denver, the students in my course and those I guest lecture to. I appreciate you trusting my voice to educate you. Thank you to the many women I have spoken to whose tears of release allowed space for my own healing. I thank you for again trusting a young woman to help guide your journey.

Last but not least, as all things come in divine and due timing, I am thankful for the entrance of the Tree into my life. When we meet spirits that remind us of who we are, we are able to become more of who we are. Thank you for all that IS.

With Gratitude,
Phoenix Kelley Jackson

Introduction

I HAVE A RADIANT AND SPIRITUALLY focused son named Simba Ausar. He is a beautiful and grounded version of his father and me. I always joked around that he was a derivative of me from the neck up and a representative of his father everywhere else. He carries my unlimited and magnanimous way of thinking. His spirit radiates as a replication of my own. Ever since he could speak he has said very 'deep' things. These things often forced you to pause and think about what just exited from his spirit.

The earliest memory I have of him 'saying' something with conviction was when he was a tiny 5 months old. His father would pick him up and send him slowly soaring in the air in the airplane fashion. This day, his father raised him up high two times in a row. This made Simba cough. He was obviously uncomfortable and wanted to express it so.

His father asked him, "Do you want to do it again?"

He profusely shook his head side to side conveying, "NO!"

We all burst into laughter, because not only was this little guy expressing himself in a yes or no fashion, we had no idea he understood the concept of yes or no just yet.

His father asks him again, "DO YOU WANT TO DO IT AGAIN??"

Simba looked very pointedly at his father and shook his head "NOOOO" even faster once again and then swung his hand to hit his father's arm to further drive home his point that he did not want to be flown in the air at that moment. He spoke with conviction through his body language. His clarity of expression started then.

I have another memory of him being 3 years old. We spent the holidays out in California with extended family. The fireplace was brewing, holiday music rang through the sound speakers, and everyone sat on the couch just talking and sharing space.

Simba kept looking into the fire. He then walks over to his Grandmother and says, "Grandma Nana... What do you see in the fire?"

She took a pause, a few minutes pass, then she responds, "I do not know what I see in the fire Simba...."

He replies, "Grandma Nana I see _____ in the fire." (What he saw in the fire had no name so the title of it was inaudible.) And then he began to express what the fire looked like to him.

A magical and very present child he is, as all our children are.

During an interesting transition in my journey I needed this child's wisdom and foresight. I had so much coming at me and so many things happening around me that I felt groundless. I was in constant flight, both literally and figuratively. So much so that I started to become confused with what my own purpose was. A purpose that I carved out of the ashes years prior.

Ausar was 9 years old. He was still the same vibration, except now he loved football and was a super manifestor. Anything he wanted somehow appeared before him. I walked over to him one day and gave him a forehead kiss and a strong hug and told him that I needed to ask him a question.

"What do you think my purpose is? What do you think I was brought onto this Earth for? What do you think I was meant to do?"

He told me to allow him to think about it. I was on pins and needles waiting for him to return.

Five minutes later he returned to my bedroom and said, "Nana, you are here to MOLD PEOPLE TO BE POWERFUL. I hear you on the phone and on the radio, at the college, and while you speak. You always are telling people about what they can do in business and in life. You are always helping them get better and when they are done talking to you they go out and do even bigger things!"

He said this with such conviction just as I had witnessed him for the first time at 5 months expressing his discontent with the moment. He looked at me like I should have already known this truth and then he scurried off to play as if he did not just change my life.

His conviction and clarity into my journey birth this book. From this book, I give you the blueprint of finding your journey into your purpose. Allow The Spirit of Business to be your voice of clarity as it has been for me. Let's dive in.

"Your time is limited, so don't waste it living someone else's life. Don't be trapped by dogma – which is living with the results of other people's thinking. Don't let the noise of others' opinions drown out your own inner voice. And most important, have the courage to follow your heart and intuition. They somehow already know what you truly want to become. Everything else is secondary."

— ***Steve Jobs***

SECTION 1

SO, YOU WANT TO START A BUSINESS?

CHAPTER 1

PURPOSE

So, you want to start a business?

Or so you want to change your life?

Or so you want to create something?

Or so you want to change your career path?

However you view the question, the answer is within. This book is not just for those seeking to become an entrepreneur but for anyone seeking answers surrounding making a leap to the next phase of their life especially pertaining to their creative output and how they want to present their talents to the world.

What is your purpose for starting this new endeavor? Is it money, fame, to serve, or do you simply have something to offer to others? No matter what age you are, there is an audience, there is someone who wants what you have to offer and there is someone who needs you and your authenticity. Whatever your reasons, make sure that it is positive and not based on what others think or how others have treated you in the past. Never create or move through life with the revenge or "I will show them" attitude. Bad foundational seeds lead to unhealthy organizational culture. Let your desires and actions within and around your life be as pure as possible. This will ensure a firm foundation upon which to create.

While you are questioning why you want to start something new, it can be quite normal not to come up with the perfect answer. Sometimes it is not always about the initial questions, "So I want to start a business, where do I begin and what do I want to do?" However it is about honing in on your thoughts and digging up the correct questions. Based on your needs and desires at this point in your life your question may be transformed into:

How might I start over?

How might I begin again although I have been doing XYZ for so long?

What do I want to do with my life?

What do I have to offer?

How might I move into a better economic situation?

How can I keep up with those around me or how can I better serve those around me?

Each of these questions can be seen as problems, and with every problem there is a solution. In thinking on starting a business (or making a life change) the focus ought not be on the question but the problems in which you are wanting to solve. If your problem revolves around not being happy at your day to day job then the solution will entail finding avenues to remove youself out of that position as soon as possible. When you are thinking about any life changes and adjustments you have to ruminate on, "What will be the benefit of making this change?"

If you believe that you want to start a business to satisfy your need of exiting the workforce, starting a business will be just one of the many solutions you could use to satisfy that need. Then you will need to open up your eyes to other ways in which you can satisfy that need or problem and explore the options. View the diagrams below for a clearer explanation:

For example: overtime you have realized that you want to leave your current job but you are not sure what to do next. You have to take a different course and transform your question into one of benefit. What would it benefit me to leave my job?

Your belief is that you want to like what you do (and make money doing it.) So, the new question is, "How might I gain more income and like what I do?" The options are the answers to leaving your current position.

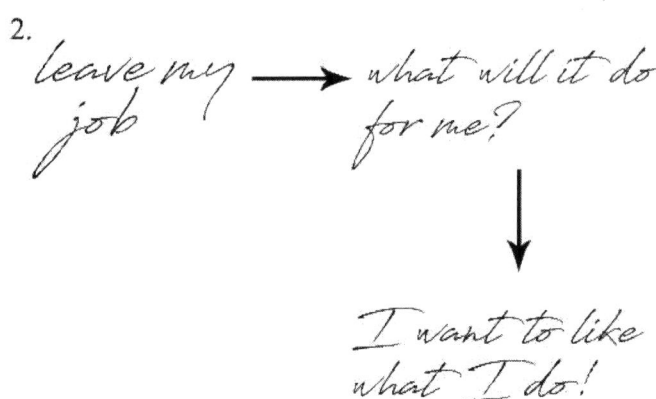

Now you can have an open mind of the options ahead and act accordingly. You are now no longer stuck with the idea of leaving a job, you are within expanded awareness of the many avenues you can take to reach your ultimate goal of liking what you do. When you are given a wide range of solutions, it aides in you being unstuck on any given issue or problem. Being aware of where you want change in your life and where you seek solutions is the utmost important step to beginning the journey into entrepreneurship or lifelong change.

3. New question:
   How might I gain more income and like what I do?

   ↓ leave my job
   ↓ online tools
   ↓ start a business
   ↓ and more...

CHAPTER 2

ACCEPTANCE. COMMITMENT. OPTIMISM.

F ROM THIS POINT FORWARD anything you say or do either moves you closer to or away from your vision of your expanded life. Let's first start by having compassion for and *acceptance* for WHERE YOU ARE RIGHT NOW! Yes, right now... whether that is in your bed reading this book, tea in hand or while you are in a chair, contemplating your next step. Where you are right now is all there is. This is an important step before we dive into this book. Know that where you are is simply... where you are and where you are supposed to be. I know that you may have heard this before, but this is a tough concept to embody. If you were meant to be someplace else you would be. The curves, bumps, delays, flights, red carpet rides, super highs and super lows all manifested and strengthened your character within. Through time, that tenacious presence that you are will manifest into wisdom. Wisdom-- that which is seldom gathered without experience. So, honor and appreciate the experience that has led you to right NOW! You would not be YOU without it.

As we begin digging into the purpose of our journey and uncovering what we want to do and express to the world, our second need is to *com-*

mit to the journey. Become a catalyst for your own growth and development. You can alter your future significantly by committing to honor the voice inside that wants to create, build, and explore all of the possibilities ahead. Let's say it together: "I COMMIT TO MYSELF AND THE JOURNEY AHEAD." Repeat. When your mind becomes unfocused and all you want to focus on are the perceived obstacles in the way, remember that you made a commitment to yourself and you need to honor that above all else. Please stay committed, you deserve it.

Lastly but not least, we as humans are learning to recognize the relationship between our thoughts and our physical world. What we *think* directly affects how we feel and what we create around us. Your point of view of yourself and your dreams are of the utmost importance. An *optimistic* outlook is just as important. It lifts you, changes the energy you carry and elevates your vibration in preparation for what is next. We know that with the current state of the world, it is a bit tough to obtain a positive outlook. However, let's do the best we can to not confuse our Own minds and heart as it relates to our Own needs and desires within our Own journey. I keep emphasizing 'Own' because this is truly about you. What you create is about you. What you express to the world is about you. Where there is conflict between our intention (what we want or will to do) and our emotions (what we feel about what we want or will to do) little can happen and little does happen. Rid yourself of the conflict now.

Acceptance of the past journey, *commitment* to the present, and *optimism* of the journey ahead are the pillars for creating success in anything that you do, from this moment forward.

Chapter 3

INTUITION

It is time to use your intuition! What is intuition you may ask? It is something that everyone has, it is something that everyone can use and it is something that is useful to everyone in multiple ways. Intuition is the use of an extra sense outside of the physical 5 senses that we all use more readily ie hearing, tasting, touching, seeing, and smelling. Those individuals who use their 6th sense of intuition (in whatever way it manifest) tend to be more successful than those individuals who take everything in front of them as truth and as reality. Intuition tends to show up in many ways including but not exclusive to meaningful dreams, premonitions/visions, spirit seers, clairvoyance, and general external perception. These expressions of intuition lead to hunches, inspiration, subtle and sudden clarity.

Ever been driving and you pull up behind someone who has a bumper sticker or a license plate that makes sense to what you were thinking about or experiencing at that moment? Ever took a moment and thought about someone and they suddenly contact you or you run into them shortly thereafter? These types of happenings are not accidents or coincidences. It is your spirit displaying something to your mind that it knows will sway you to think or act differently concerning your next steps forward. It is letting you know that you have everything to do with manifesting your surroundings. Many people do not listen and pay attention to these moments.

Have you ever taken the time to look through a tarot deck of cards? Tarot is an ancient form of fortune telling in which the predictor uses a deck of cards, either specially designed, an archaic deck, or even a general deck of playing cards. The suits and numbers all have a meaning. The very first card shows itself as the "Joker" or in the tarot deck, the "Fool". The Fool symbolizes the individual person or spirit that is blown by the winds of change. They are the person who flows with the experiences around them unaware of really where they are going and how they are getting there. It is stated in the Bible that God takes care of children and fools. I believe that like the *Main Ingredient* song says, "Everybody plays the fool sometimes." The Fool does not necessarily pay attention to their 6th sense as they are too busy being moved through the journey instead of being a part of the development of the journey.

We tend to move aimlessly through circumstances without foresight and strategy. It is a cure for cool things to happen, as blessings tend to manifest around individuals who are bright in energy. They are lit to attract nice experiences, and at times they are dim and they attract negative experiences. However, without a desired end goal, they will not necessarily manifest the desired result of a successful business. Our goal in life is to at least learn to have forward thinking and progressive ideals on how and who we want to be (internally). How we want to live and how we want to interact with the world is secondary. While at many junctures in our lives we will not see which direction we are supposed to turn, we should work on being able to listen intently to the taps and whispers of our inner selves and of the guides around us. We must use our intuition. We should work at becoming Fool proof. Pay attention to the bumper stickers.

To step out of the role of the Fool you should first admit that you have been there. You can also pat yourself on the back because if you are reading this book then you are already in a transformative state of being and thus are already shifting out of the Fool role.

When it comes to intuition and using it to carve your own business path, the next step is Self Trust. Oh TRUST, what a loaded word. It makes us think of any situation where we have opened ourselves up and were disappointed by the experiences at hand. Well what I have learned thru my years in business is that I have had to deal with individuals who do not have a problem trusting others (they obviously trusted me to help them build their business or public image); they have had a problem trusting themselves and trusting their thoughts and feelings about their present and their future. This questioning usually has everything to do with their past. The past can be such a bitch, if we look at it that way of course. It is hard to listen to our own intuition if we have multiple layers of jarred filters covering our eyes from seeing the highest potential in what is right in front of us today.

Before we can start thinking about the path to success we have to clear the inner path so that we can begin the true journey to become who we want to become.

Please make a list of at least 3 situations or individuals that have made you question your trust of yourself or of others. Have you made any decisions or experienced things that made you wonder about your own judgment of character or your own integrity?

_____

_____

_____

_____

_____

_____

_____

_____

_____

_____

How do you think these things above have clouded your ability to trust, hear and feel your intuition moving forward?

_____

_____

_____

_____

_____

_____

_____

We are going to do some Intuitive Healing around these issues listed above. For the next 2 weeks (in the midst of continuing to read this book) I would like for you to grab hold of each situation and cleanse it. It is time to trust yourself again.

Road map to intuitive healing:

Issue 1:_____

Day 1: Write down the entire experience in the form of a letter. A letter to yourself, a letter to the person who broke your trust, etc. Fold it and sit it in a place that you could access it later. That's it.

Day 2: Find the letter and burn it (this is symbolic of the power of the moment being released from you and sent away.) As you burn it think about how you wish that situation would have turned out, release any expectations of that past circumstance, as it was MEANT to transpire the exact way that it did.

Day 3: Sit and write down what you are going to do differently in the next situation that you find yourself in. What forms of self preservation, self protection and/or compassion will you conjure up so that you can attract a better circumstance?

Day 4: Meditation and/or prayer. Some have a hard time in meditating. Some think too deeply about it and think that it is something difficult to do. Truth is... (pause and hear me clearly) ... it is the easiest thing to do. My now 11 year old has been doing it for 8 years, why? Because he was fortunate enough not to have the thoughts that it was something that he couldn't do to begin with. It is another practice just like eating and sleeping. It is a way of life. He has no blockages or filters telling him otherwise and you shouldn't either.

6 step meditation practice to rid yourself of the Fool within and to tap into your intuition.

1. Shut off every electronic around you.
2. Find a quiet place to sit or lay comfortably. (You do not have to be in Hindu/Indian style.)

3. Close your eyes.
4. Take long deep breaths. Try not to count them.
5. Allow every thought and sensation to float by like clouds in the sky. They are just that, nothing but fabrications and creations from your very busy mind. Do not allow them to rain on you. DO not grab hold to these thoughts either. In this moment, what your mind is doing has nothing to do with you.
6. Start with a 5-minute interval.

The more you do this, the easier it becomes and the quieter your mind becomes. Try 5 minutes to start and then every week amp it up another 5 minutes. If you can meditate as often as you can remember, your world will be a more balanced and peaceful place. Trust me on this one. It works. You will feel resistance to doing this as it is a new discipline that the mind has to learn but do not allow your mind to control you. It is your mind, it belongs to you. Own it. Repeat entire process for all 3 trust issues. Be gentle with yourself and take time to really process the effects of the things that you have experienced with others.

Some believe that time heals all things (yeah right). I know individuals that are still angry after 20 years over a very old wound. Clarity heals all things! I have witnessed and experienced instant healing from circumstances once I understood it and understood its placement within my journey. I understood the "why" of the situation. *(But Phoenix, I still don't know why these things happened.)* My response to this statement is to think about it and meditate on it until you find clarity and unravel it. Do not think about it until you find clarity, meditate on it until you find clarity. Unravel the situation by asking yourself the right questions in your moments of meditation. For example, let's say that you were in a situation where you lost all of your financial savings by the hands of someone else. Think on how that transpired, what you could have done differently, and what you GAINED from the experience.

The blessings are in the lessons of every circumstance. The difference is that when you meditate on it you are seeing the experience as an observer and not as a participant. You are placing space around the experience in order to see it with as much objectivity as possible. Then you use this same objectivity to analyze how your life is different because of that experience. Every circumstance has a place, has a purpose, and is a part of an extended game plan beyond what we can see and feel. Tap into that.

It becomes easier to carve a path of success when you are carrying clarity in your back pocket and better yet when you have a healthy level of self trust and self acceptance for what has happened and for what will happen. We are indeed able to hear ourselves; we are able to listen to the next steps as ALL ANSWERS ARE FROM WITHIN. We already know what we are supposed to do, we just have a hard time listening and even when we listen, most of us have a hard time embodying what we hear! Don't be that person... Don't be a Fool. All in all, using your intuition brings clarity and clarity heals everything else.

SECTION 2

DIGGING IN

CHAPTER 4

THE SPIRIT OF BUSINESS

ON THIS BEAUTIFUL HOME that we reside called Earth, many believe what they choose to believe. Many believe what they have been taught to believe and many believe what they know to be true through experience. Would we all agree that we as humans on this Earth have five sensory tools that we carry (at minimum)? Most of us are born physically able to hear, taste, see, touch, and smell. Through these mechanisms we can take in and experience our world. We are able to live and interact with moments that occur in front of and around us. These senses were created for us to perceive our physical reality better.

So what occurs when we have 'feelings' that surface that are outside of our immediate sensory capabilities? What are these moments? Why are these moments happening? If we take a step deeper, there are other sensory that we carry, *alternative powers* I call them. I believe as well as I know to be true that humans are evolving to be able to converge their lowest (our five sensory self) and their highest (multi sensory self.) This higher self or multi-sensory self I call the Spirit. The ability to absorb and perceive our world on a very elevated level in which our human body is at one with our physical world and those within it is a great thing. There is an invisible bubble of energy that we all carry around and within us. It is within that bubble our spirit, our aura, and/or our soul exist. These are one in the same.

So, what is the spirit?

Before we were birth into this physical body, we were an energy and a consciousness waiting to be born onto this Earth to experience everything we could at this level. The spirit is the invisible eternal aspect of yourself. Before we were birth we (outside of any physical form) were a manifestation of Divine Intelligence that was waiting to have the ability to live, create and evolve on Earth. You are not separate from the spirit that you originated from just because you are now living in a physical form.

Let's put this into practice as to not get confused. Have you ever walked into a room and stood next to someone and felt uncomfortable all of a sudden? Or have you ever looked into someone's eyes and you two felt the same thing at the same time or your kindred connection was on such a level that you felt that you must've known this person in the past? Except there is no past, you have never known this person in this life before that moment. I believe in these moments are when you are connecting with someone's spirit. Your invisible eternal self is in tandem with their invisible eternal self. Your experience feels fated. Or you have those times when you are repelled away from someone for no apparent reason although you do not know them. In these moments, we cannot blame our reaction on surface biases. It is deeper than that. Consequently, there is something that you sense that does not vibrate with you.

There are some individuals with whom you surround yourself with who feel great to you, they make you happy near and far because their energy or vibration is one that you sense is healthy, aligned and clear. Humans such as the Dalai Lama, Ghandi, Christ, ancient and modern leaders, Oprah, Pema Chodron, Malcolm X and more, are all individuals who are or were moving with aligned spirits. If they were to stand next to you, the clarity of them living their purpose would make you feel good because it is radiating within their aura. At some point in their life, their spirit activated and took over their mind and movement, to place them on a flow of high intention in which they would positively affect the world. It was their responsibility to do so. They understood what they were here to do. They lived or are living out their purpose in service of those around them. The decisions that you make in this life help you evolve and aids your spirit in being present. Present and high spirits attract present and high spirits.

What does this mean 'being present'? In this day and age most humans are walking around as the walking dead. Meaning that most are walking around using just their ears, eyes, nose, hands, and mouth to experience the world around them and a nice amount of us on this planet indulge in various forms of drugs and chemical catalyst to numb even those senses. We drink alcohol, smoke and indulge in tobacco products, and engage in many forms of 'feel good' agents. The human that can bypass just the normal experience and whom can use their body as a vehicle to experience but who meditates, centers themselves and becomes one with their spirit self are the humans who are going to be fulfilled on Earth. Nothing can replace that level of fulfillment. No drug will help you find it. Your spirit can sense an empty person surrounded by all the material comforts that the world has to offer as well as it can sense the joyous and warm heart underneath a tough and aggressive exterior. It can sense wealth within poverty and poverty within riches. Our goal is to live out our expression and to co-create with others who do the same.

Wisdom, compassion and love are all products of the spirit. Our spirit being the immortal and eternal entity that it is, its work is never done. It is here to positively manipulate the experiences that you have so that you can become more of It and less of the physical presence that you are. Your spirit knows best and once your body is long gone, it will transition into its next form or a formless state carrying the beautiful power and manifestations that you have yielded in this life. Your spirit craves to express itself through you and will fade into a still version of itself if you allow your mind/ego to stay in control of your five-sensory reality. Everything that happens in your life either takes you closer or further away from a full expression of your spirit. You decide and with every decision that you make in life, especially large ones, you have to think... How will this affect my spirit? If you are thinking about marriage, think, will this person service my spirit? Does this person raise the highest form of expression out of me? Does this person help grow and heal me? Or does this person only support my pursuit of material things and obtaining a false sense of lifelong fulfillment? Most marriages in America fail because mutual evolution of the spirit does not occur (amongst many other reasons.)

Everything has a spirit. Everything has a spirit as everything is made of energy. Everything that is on this planet whether organic or manmade has a vibration and is meant with a certain intention in mind. Some intentions are meant to be experienced by living creatures and some things are meant for observation (like the Moon.) Either way it has a spirit. Moments and experiences have spirits as well. How can that be? It is easy. Take a moment and imagine your favorite color. How does that color make you feel? When was the last time that you did something that made you extremely happy? What was your last great experience? Now imagine that your favorite color was flowing around and through you during those moments. You experienced the spirit of that moment. Most of our great moments, even our day to day hum drum moments are here to teach us something as we interact with them. When you are in a high flowing and energetic spiritual moment, many more follow behind it, one great moment after the next. You are therefore living within the spirit of each moment.

The big question: What does spirit have to do with business? The spirit has everything to do with business! *Any and every business is nothing but a reflection of a person's need to express themselves or their purpose.* Albeit some have good purposes and others have purposes that involve greed and harming others through their expression. Every single business has a vibration that it carries and that vibration has a way in which it interacts with its immediate environment. There is no one single description for what the spirit of a particular business is (you will have to determine that as you evolve your business.) However, the Spirit of Business is one of mercantile servitude. What does this mean? Every spirit has a purpose correct? Well most, if not all businesses have the purpose to be of service to the public in one way or another. In that fulfillment of purpose, businesses exchange finances or other forms of payment like barter. Whether a business provides a service or product, it is a thought, energy and a creation that began in the mind of an individual. Whether it is a solopreneur that decides to provide knowledge and a service to the public or someone with a high level of ingenuity who thinks of a way to change the landscape of communication and human interaction ie Steve Jobs. Jobs created and spearheaded Apple Inc. Does Apple have a spirit to it that is fulfilling and purpose driven? You damn right it does and anyone and everyone who purchases an Apple product interacts with that spirit.

As you take the time to examine what your spirit means to you and how your spirit would like to express itself through you, also think about in what way can you provide for yourself by doing so? As an entrepreneur, you also have to make a living in this financially driven reality in which we reside. This is a fact. So not only do you have to dig deeper into who you are, but you also have to figure out what you would like to express that can make you a living. Simple right? As we dive into this book we will examine ways to accomplish this.

CHAPTER 5

INTUITION II

ONE DOES NOT HAVE TO BE Marvel Comic's Spider Man to have heightened spider senses. We all have them and we all use them in various ways. For example, have you ever been in a dangerous situation where you just knew something was getting ready to happen that was not going to be ok? No? Ok maybe that is a bit extreme. Simply put, have you ever been in a situation where something told you that something just wasn't right? Your instincts knew that things were a bit shifty around you, so you reacted on those instincts by either leaving the space you were in or speaking out about it or if you are cool, calm and collected person who thinks that they can handle everything, you stood around and waited to see what was actually going to happen. These are our spider senses or in more spiritual terms, our intuition.

We speak about intuition throughout this book as it is one of my personal super powers. As previously stated, your intuition is a gift from your spirit that lends you support when your five senses fail you. Sometimes our mind cannot give rational reason as to why we know something or why we perceive something accurately in any given moment. This is nothing but your intuition. Wise and compassionate awareness is open and available to everyone. Yes everyone. Our insights do not come from our regular physical senses. They are filtered through our spirit and reflected and made rational through our intuition. Then we are supposed to act. Some believe intuition and hunches are brought to us by the ancestors, external spirits, guides, angels or simply from within.

Why don't more people listen to their intuition? Yes, it is due to a lack of self trust but it also has to do with layers of doubt and second guessing of things that are right in front of them. It is quite easy to become stagnant throughout life as it pertains to doubt. Once we have been through a multitude of circumstances that did not turn out the way that we may have intended, many of us start to question things every step of the way instead of allowing ourselves to respond without filters to life. We do not allow things to unfold as intended. Let's dive deeper into this thing called doubt, because if we carry doubt we will never listen to our intuition properly.

Chapter 6

THE DOUBT MONSTER

If you are like most individuals then you have two voices in your head, hold on, I am not saying that you are crazy, however we know that there are usually two sides to ourselves and these two sides often display themselves when we think we need them most. I like to call them the Higher Self and the Lower Self or the Doubt Monster! The Higher Self tends to reach in and let us know what is around the corner, it tells us to watch out when there is danger and it is the voice of wisdom, intuition and compassion for others. It is the voice that is usually kind and assists in aiding us in figuring out our next steps in life and how to navigate the toughest parts of ourselves and how to work best with those around us. The Lower Self or Doubt Monster does the exact opposite! It can mean well; The Doubt Monster thinks that it is protecting us from the things we do not see nor understand. It thinks that everything is a threat or out to get us and therefore it keeps us locked into a constant state of seeking comfort, of not taking risk, and of being in low or high levels of anxiety at all times.

Due to the instant gratification filled culture that we live in, most humans are constantly living in a state of anxiety and doubt on one level or another. Doubt is nothing but a sensation, a feeling and an emotion of uncertainty. Uncertainty is that ambiguous space that we find ourselves in when we do not know what is next or when we do not know how to create the outcome we are seeking in any given situation. Our biggest job is to face that monster and break thru it to reflect and express our highest selves as often as possible. It is not always up to us to know what is next but what we can do is fine tune our highest self so that we can do a better job of manifesting what does come next. This is an arduous process of healing that many dare not undertake. It takes courage and the ability to face up to what we fear the most. Many people simply fear how great they can become!

Doubt shows itself in so many ways but it has the same outcome: not truly creating the business of your dream or becoming as successful as you desire to be.

In the spaces below I want you to write down your largest vision for yourself that you can think of. Make it grand and make it something that you can truly envision yourself achieving. As you write it you may notice how the fear and the doubt tries to creep in, do not allow it to stop you from jotting down your highest dream! This is no holds bars, what do you want to do, who do you want to be, how do you want to affect change, what would you like to be known for during this lifetime? What would you like your legacy to be?

_____

_____

_____

_____

_____

_____

_____

_____

_____

Next, please remind yourself of WHY do you want to do what you want to do, who will you be impacting, why is it your dream?

_____

_____

_____

_____

_____

_____

_____

_____

Now time for the hard and honest truth, what has stopped your from moving towards making that vision a reality?

_____

_____

_____

_____

_____

_____

_____

_____
_____
_____

What do you think will stop you from this point forward?

_____
_____
_____
_____
_____
_____
_____
_____
_____

In the many years that I have worked for myself I have had many times in which I wanted to run off and get a corporate position. There were times when I did not know where my next project was coming from or where would the money come from to cover the multiple thousands of dollars in expenses per month. At times this caused a level of paralyzing anxiety in which I would sleep for hours in the middle of the day versus tackling the most difficult problems in front of me. The saving grace for me was when a Mother in my life named Marilyn would (on a cyclical basis) remind me of how much she believed in me and she would speak so highly of how far I have come and how far I am to go and she would remind me of how strong I was. This was what I needed to continue to move forward. I needed encouragement and the affirmation of strength from those who knew me best. She and many like her are what I would like to call "Light Bearers" – they are the mirror to you of the light that you possess in yourself and if your light seems dim or you are at a place where it is hard to see your own light, they can lend you some of theirs. We all need encouragement, inspiration, and support. There is nothing wrong with having your own cheering section when you need it most.

Make a list of at least 3 people you can reach out to when you are feeling fear and doubt who can share their light and uplift you in any given moment. You can chat with these individuals and be honest about what you may need when you are second guessing yourself. These individuals must be willing to support you when you need them, so make sure they are dependable. In the future, we do not want to use the excuse of having no support. Let's build our support system now.

_____

_____

_____

_____

_____

_____

_____

_____

_____

Now that we have an external support system, let us look at our internal support. I have ways of how to deal with the Doubt Monster within, piece by piece. Trust me, it isn't going to want to go away and at times it may try to convince you that it is gone and it will cleverly hide itself in the cellars of your heart and mind and try to find the perfect time to rear its head and ruin all that you are building. Doubt is not an easy thing to escape from, we all experience it. However how you deal with it dictates how successful you will become. These are the number one excuses that people use to not move forward and they are a feast of a meal for the Doubt Monster:

1. **"I just do not have the time."** I get it, you are a Mom or a Dad, you have a career (that you probably do not like), you have a home, obligations, TV to watch, Facebook to check, etc. There are 24 hours in a day or 168 hours in a week. We know that time is such a precious commodity and there never seems to be enough of it, unless of course you are in the DMV or on jury duty, then time is infinite or so it seems! What we prioritize, we create energy for and what we create energy for, our time expands into. The things that we are enthusiastic about, the things that feel good to us and the things that do not feel like a chore are what we NEED to put our time into. I've always stated, "I am so busy" and "I just do not have the time to do that." What I was really telling myself and others was that what they were asking of me wasn't going to happen because it was not a priority. Putting your new ideas or your new business into the category of a priority will get you that much closer to it being a success and for you to manifest that grand vision that you have for yourself! We are listening to everything around us but our inner selves which is the greatest guidance of all. Let's make time for that.

    Tackling the time excuse is about instilling discipline within your daily life. It not that there isn't enough time, we need to review how our time is allocated throughout the day. Let's put time into perspective for just a moment.... If the Earth was only 24 hours old, humans would have arrived/evolved on it only 2 minutes ago...

and in 1 second of our Earth's existence, social media and digital communication has absorbed the minds of the masses with the average person checking their phone and digital devices over 85 times a day! We spend on average 5 hours a day reading, engaging, and communicating within social media or digital communication ie online magazines, news, YouTube, etc. This may not be you, but what could you do with an extra 5 hours a day, what can you do with an extra hour per day? I know what!! Manifest the business of your dreams!

Self observation:

The best thing we can do is observe ourselves. Your next exercise over the next 2 days is calculating how much you pick up your phone or digital device (not when it rings or someone reaches to you), I want you to observe how many times you reach for it.

How many times did you reach for your phone or media device?
_____

How many hours or minutes do you estimate that you spent on it that had nothing to do with your dream?
_____

Do you think you can curve your enthusiasm for your media devices?
_____

Really?
_____

Moving forward in future chapters we are going to (yes me and you) work on shutting off the noise which will automatically create more time in your daily life.

2. **"I am too old and have no idea how to change now."** Oh isn't that cute, you think you are too old to be whatever you want to be. Remember in elementary school when your teacher said to you that you can be anything when you grow up, well guess what, it is true! Most of us are not even fully mature or grown up no matter the age. Maturity has to do with how our life path plans out and how we perceive and interact with everything around us. Is it just me or do you notice that most of the more highly successful individuals today are older and seasoned? However some of them just broke through after years of hard work or after just now getting to a fearless place. They suddenly decided to step out on their truth, worked hard, got discovered or just simply started flowing with what made them happy and their life started to fall into place effortlessly. You either go against the grain or flow with it and if you feel that you are too old it's probably because you have spent so many years within resistance and going against the grain of your true calling. Most of us spend our time resisting what is right for us for those things that feel good to our senses. We can end that excuse today! Reinvention of the self is the name of the game.

How to tackle the age excuse has everything to do with self perception. You are only as old as you feel on the inside. A family member of mine, Baba Theo, is currently 86 years old and is one of the most aligned and vibrant human beings that I believe I will ever know. I wish he could be around forever (this is how happy his presence makes me). He dances around his home and does a little shimmy here and there and eats and lives a healthy and stress-free life and do you know at what age he started this transition? He was all but a mere 64. He learned meditative techniques, changed his living and eating habits and is now one of the healthiest humans that I know. He also taught himself how to navigate the internet and the digital ocean, how to purchase the best headphones to listen to all of his favorite jazz tunes and Zen sounds on YouTube, all the while being one heck of a researcher when it is time to learn about anything spiritual and cutting edge in our modern world. And remember... he is 86.

Think about individuals such as Steve Harvey who broke thru at his peak later in his career, he is now 60+ and thriving at an incredible peak! Ellen DeGeneres received her star-studded TV show just 13 years ago at the age of 45. Rapper and entertainment mogul Jay Z/Sean Carter recorded his first album at the age of 27, in an industry where the average rap star fizzles out by then. No matter what age you are, there is an audience, there is someone who wants what you have to offer, and there is someone who needs YOU and your authenticity.

Self observation:

What do you think about when you think of your age? Are there any limitations that you see? Why?

_____
_____
_____
_____
_____
_____
_____
_____

What age would you rather be to do what you want to do?

_____

And why didn't you do these things at that age?

_____
_____
_____
_____

So how would you feel if you never accomplished what you wanted due to your age?

_____
_____
_____
_____

What is the worse that could happen if you do those things now?

_____
_____
_____
_____

3. **"I don't see the opportunity ahead of me, I can't afford to do it or simply don't know how!"** Now I am sorry to say and do not want to sound facetious but this is the most tired excuse of all! I say this because I have been piss broke with $-600.00 in my bank account and I found a way. I opened myself up to find a way and to listen to the guidance around and within me to find a way. The wonderful thing about our world is that it is exposed. There are so many ways to learn how to do and build anything you want. There is a flavor for every taste online and in books. We are in an information charged world which has its ups and downs but the upside to it is that you can find out how to do anything... this is not 1990, 80, 70... you have access. Let us repeat this: I have access. The world is flat and with that I can see above the horizon. Let's be honest, life isn't fair and everyone is born on differing playing fields even those born to the same household. I have a true belief that the worse the start the more triumph is the finish. People who have it easy, struggle with figuring out what their true purpose is and who they truly are, they have to learn character development and the meaning of life living in the bounds of material entrapment. People who are born of meager circumstances have to struggle with figuring out what their true purpose is and who they truly are, they have to learn character development and the meaning of life living in the bounds of a lack of material belongings. The point is that everyone is seeking very similar things; we all need the same basic levels of protection, balance, security and contentment. We can fight the environment from which we came or understand that our duty is to change it to become what we think it ought to be. Going to your immediate network to start your search for a mentor or instilling discipline that you are going to research one person and their life's journey to see how

they made it are both great steps to take. You will be surprised to know that NO ONE did it alone. Everyone has needed a leg up and for someone to assist them and to give them a lift towards their desired destination. It is ok to ask for what you seek and to ask for assistance. Most individuals would be happy to help you along your way.

Self-observation:

What limitations do you see on yourself? If it is money, what can you cut out of your life to make space for saving and making more? For example, ridding yourself of none necessities like cable TV, eating out often, living in a space that is too much for you or driving a car that cost too much to maintain.

_____
_____
_____
_____
_____

Growing up, did you ever hear any *limiting verbiage* around you? Did someone plant seeds of self destruction? Or worse did you see a parent or guardian who displayed subpar qualities and characteristics or who did not fulfill any dreams of their own?

_____
_____
_____
_____
_____

What characteristics have you adopted from others or that you carry within yourself that hinder you from attracting or creating the resources you need to start and maintain your desired enterprise? Think deeply about this, many of us are replicated products of our childhood environment and our immediate surroundings, whether we want to admit it or not.

_____

_____

_____

_____

_____

As you take the time to examine the excuses and levels of doubt that you carry, do not be afraid of what can surface emotionally. It can sometimes be a painful process. All of us are dealing with something and have bags of crap that we are carrying. The bags get heavier and heavier as the years go by and we even convince ourselves that they do not exist. Not examining the doubt we carry will alter our intentions in a direction in which we do not want them to go. One step at a time, all it takes is one step at a time.

Take time to think about you have allowed the Doubt Monster to win. Most of us are 0-55. You took an "L" (for loss) for every year that you denied the world of your expression and denied yourself from creating.

SECTION 3

FIGURING IT OUT

CHAPTER 7

INTENTION

MOST INDIVIDUALS DO NOT MOVE through life with intention. Many of us operate on a mechanical level. Doubt can and will do that to you. We wake up and go to work and try to focus on the things that we need to do. We focus on our family, our jobs, our hobbies, and the things that entertain us. How you feel, how you think, and how you act is a reflection of your life's intentions. What is an intention? An intention is not only a desire but it is a plan or a purpose. When one has an intention in mind, their actions align with that intention, or so it should. There are times in life where one has a desire to have a situation or circumstance go in a certain direction, however their thoughts and actions do not align to that intention. In high fashion, the end result that occurs is quite different from what was originally desired. It is extremely important to check your intentions. What do you really want?

There are conscious or subconscious intentions that are continuously swirling around in our minds and hearts. Things tend to align in our lives when there is a mergence of these various intentions or when we realize and make sense out of what we truly desire out of life. Every decision that you make and every experience that you have is a reflection of your intention. I am a firm believer that nothing in our life happens without our conscious or subconscious consent. Nothing. I know that this is a tough concept to grasp because it really places the onus of the good, the bad and the ugly that happens in our life on our own shoulders. As someone who has experienced the good, the bad and the ugly, I accept the onus and growth that was gained from such experiences. It is such a responsibility to shoulder. However, when we understand how powerful this truth is, we can then begin to match our intentions and our experiences to elevate us to a better way of living and being.

Phoenix, I spent years of my life behind bars, how did I ask for this? (Bars being metaphorical. Bars can be literal or figurative.) We all at some point have felt the weight of being behind bars. Either growing up in a chaotic environment as a child, being in damaging relationships, having positions that drained the life out of us, or being caught in a way of life that is not of our choosing. Some on Earth are born in war torn countries. This is outside of their control. These are bars. Some are born to drug addicted parents and some are born behind bars in our massive and generational ingesting prison system in the US. I believe those that are born in low vibration or painful environments decided before they came into this world that they needed that experience in order to grow and evolve their soul. I believe that we are born where we are supposed to be when we are supposed to be and no spirit on this planet is here happenstance. Our spirit knows what conditions that it needs to crystallize itself. It knows what it needs to become a diamond out of a coal. It knows what it needs to evolve. Some who are extremely powerful must go through some extreme circumstances to realize who they are and why they are here.

For example, in the US, the Black American male is under constant scrutiny. He is both feared and emulated, not because he will harm or kill someone (which is the blanket excuse for oppressing him) but he is feared because he is considered to be too powerful if he stands within his greatness. He is emulated because he created multiple levels of creation and expression that is being duplicated around the world, even while expressing his lower self and being bred in subpar environments. Imagine what he can do if he had every tool available to him. This is what his counterpart fears. There are men who do not want the competition so they withhold tools, knowledge and resources from each other and particularly the Black male. They put more money into prisons than schools and create conditions in which the Black male has a hard time surviving let alone learning how powerful his true nature is. So what does this mean from the victim's perspective (the Black male)? It means that under the horrible conditions and environment that he is born, his soul has to evolve and so it requested such conditions to force it to take back the power in which it has given away in previous generations. This is a huge subject that I just tapped into however it is real. Individuals who are diamonds, but who have been reduced to coal must take on the pressure and respond to it and be the catalyst for itself unsheathing as a diamond. Are you ready to become a diamond? How much pressure do you need to become one?

This can be examined further when one looks at the state of women around the world. Women deal with some form of oppression and degradation in even the most evolved countries. Religion, spirituality, and the ego have all been the main excuses used to oppress women throughout history. As there is a new term that is being expressed, "The Future is Female;" women are learning to take back their power and are learning to express the pain that they have experienced from the male counterparts. They would have never learned how powerful the culmination of their strength was if they had not experienced what it was like to have their strength diminished.

You too have to take a concerted role in becoming your own diamond self. Look at your circumstances no matter how harsh they seem. They are the contrast that you have needed to become a better version of yourself.

When you start moving with intention and purpose every day, you begin to heal and merge yourself into being who you were meant to be despite all else. So how does one reconcile their subconscious intentions and those that are their surface intentions? Since intention is the beginning of every vision, every dream and consequently every business, it when used properly is the greatest power used to manifest all that we desire. Every experience and deed begins with intention.

"You are what your deepest desire is. As your desire is, so is your intention. As your intention is, so is your will. As your will is, so is your deed. As your deed is, so is your destiny." – Upanishads, Vedic text.

One law within figuring out and properly funneling your true intentions are planting the thought of them in your mind and then releasing them to grow and develop. Below are 4 ways to start to align yourself with your intention.

1. With the noisiness in our world it is so tough to quiet our mind to see only what *we* truly desire. We look at social media and the television and envision what everyone else has and what everyone else is experiencing and it makes it hard to take note of what we really want. Before bed take some time to say to yourself, "What are my deepest desires and true intentions for myself?" and lay down before bed for ten minutes and just allow yourself to drift into sleep with this thought on your mind. With the way the Universe, God, your guides work, you will start to see things happen around you and in your dreams that will start to display for you what you really desire. Pay attention.

2. Since intention are more powerful when you are in a happy or content state, I always say it is better to ask for what you want

when you are within a state of appreciation already. Individuals that are naysayers or who have something negative to feel or think about what you want are people who do not need to be in your sphere. Your spirit knows what you need and those people will fall away as you continue to build upon your positive intentions. Do whatever you need to do to keep yourself in a feel-good mode.

3. Detachment is a huge emotion that many do not talk about. Having indifference will make a difference! Once you have stated your intentions and figured them out... let them go. Say goodbye to the intention and do what you need to do to prepare to receive that intention! When we are so attached to something happening the way we want it to happen, 9 times out of 10 it will not happen that way. A lot of times we see a straight line to our dreams not knowing that our personal evolution requires a zig zag to that destination. Many times when we are attached to something we carry fear with us along the way. Think about that time when you really wanted a relationship or friendship to work out, so much so that you overdid something along the way to usher it to that end, all to watch it crumble anyhow. More success happens when we do the mechanical work and allow spaces to evolve or spirit to grow the intention.

What do you want? I mean really? What do you really want? What are your deepest desires?

Let's start off by thinking about where we want to be in 3 years and in 5 years. Write down what your desired life looks and feels like.

In 3 years I want to be:

_____

_____

_____

_____

_____

In 5 years I want to be:

_____

_____

_____

_____

In 10 years I want to be:

_____

_____

_____

_____

In 20 years I want to be:

_____

_____

_____

_____

In the future, the following individuals are in my life:

_____

_____

_____

_____

_____

In the future, daily, I walk around feeling like:

_____

_____

_____

_____

_____

When we picture ourselves in the future, it is a powerful manifestation. We see who we want to be and where we want to be. We can start to place ourselves down a trajectory of becoming that person. Timing is truly everything and everyone's timing is different. We are not in a race to get anywhere fast. We are on a course to evolve in this life. If you have opposing intentions in your heart and mind, you will create a diametrically opposed reality. Many individuals who you see in conflict with their life and themselves are living and breathing within dual intentions. You do not want to be that person. Take time to get clear about your trajectory at all cost. If one intention (that is not positive) is stronger than the positive one then that is the one that will manifest. If and when you are clear within your intentions. Once you sit back and allow it to, it will evolve your current environment. You will turn around and notice how certain circumstances have occurred that you weren't even expecting. You will notice how opportunity came peaking around the corner and before it knocked on the door, you were there waiting to open it.

SECOND LAYER INTENTIONS

When we are looking at intentions, we must understand that there are layers to this. You are the first tier of importance within the manifestations of powerful intention. If you are not aligned with where you want to be, you will not have the type of affect on your immediate environment as you would otherwise. Your personal intentions are the utmost important and next are the intentions of those that you are responsible for.

My second layer of intention goes to my son and the children within my immediate family. Growing up neither of my parents made conscious effort to build a legacy for the next generation. This was the case mainly because they were not taught to obtain and maintain financial freedom from their parents. At times if we are not careful we pass down generational thoughts and intentions just through sheer identification. We not only pass down our genetics but also learned habits and behaviors. As we think about our next layer of intentions we have to consider these things. We have to think about the habits, thoughts and behaviors we are passing along to our children, our dependants, our co-workers, our employees, etc. As I stated, my son Ausar is my priority. I realized many years ago that if I were alone and had no dependants, my life would be extremely different. I don't want many things, I don't need many things. My lists of material desires are very limited. Once I had a child, I realized the importance of legacy. My first tier of intention intertwines intricately with my second tier. My intention is to create a legacy for future generations to build upon.

With whom does your second layer of intention rest upon? And Why?

_____

_____

_____

_____

_____

How do you think you would feel when and if you are to fulfill your intentions for your second layer of individuals?

_____

_____

_____

_____

_____

Name one thing you are willing to do differently today to fulfill an intention that will impact yourself and your second tiers within the next three years?

_____

_____

_____

_____

_____

Chapter 8

WHAT NOT TO DO

You ever heard of to do list? Yes those either written out or typed out, on a sheet of paper or in a booklet, or on one's phone or to be checked off or crossed off. To do list are an awesome way at setting intentional task for the day. What about creating a list of *What Not To Do?* It was a strange thought when I first discovered this form of reverse psychology. Why don't we make a list of the things that we shouldn't do on a regular basis? Let's look deeper into how cool this concept actually is.

During our present age, it is so easy to get bogged down and inundated with life. The news, the distractions and just the overall noise can keep you feeling like you are on a race to nowhere. What it also does is makes you forget about how bad certain habits are. What if you created a cool list of 5 not to dos and pasted it up on your wall or at work in an area where you can always keep an eye on it? There will be a constant reminder to stay on course to what means most. As you look at your 'not to do list,' do not get emotionally attached to it. You are not placing your energy into the list, you are just manifesting more discipline by taking a friendly glimpse of it every now and then.

Make a list of 5 not to dos or 5 things that you will stop doing habitually in order to have more time and energy to manifest your intentions.

1. _____

2. _____

3. _____

4. _____

5. _____

Chapter 9

MOVEMENT WITHIN AWARENESS

EMPATHY IS A WONDERFUL STRENGTH to have. If every person possessed it, this world would truly be a better place. Empathy or someone who is an Empath is someone who can relate to, feel or share the emotions of others. They can feel when someone is happy, sad or somewhere in between. They also have a knack for placing themselves in someone else's shoes. Seeing both sides of the argument comes easy. In order to create an ideal business or enterprise one must be socially aware. Social awareness carries with it the responsibility to be empathic of other's needs and desires. How will you be able to provide efficiently if you are not in touch with what is happening around you? You have to be in tune both near and far. Part of this improvement starts with being a better listener (of yourself and others.)

One of my earliest tests in listening to myself and becoming more aware of what I truly desired was in the seventh grade... yes the seventh grade. My English teacher asked us to illustrate a self portrait that showed where we would be twenty years from that point. To reflect, since I was 5 years old I had told my parents that I wanted to be a doctor.

That decision was based on the fact that I had seen images on television late at night of starving African children. There were always infomercials trying to raise money for these youth. I always questioned whether the money actually made it to those villages and to those children. I digress. At the age of 5 I said that I was going to become a doctor and get rich and then go to Africa and grow food for these hungry babies. In the seventh grade during this particular exercise, I sat there and thought about how can I help those kids I saw on TV many years ago? I literally thought... *It takes too many years to become a doctor; I want to get richer sooner so I can help them faster. I want to own a business...* I drew a picture of myself with my hair up in a conservative 'business bun', with my arms crossed, with buildings up behind me with my first name in big bright letters at the top of the buildings. That is what I truly wanted. I wanted to become a powerful and successful business owner.

The circle of this experience is that many years later my face was on a banner of a website I was featured on with the skyline of Denver behind me. Now, none of those buildings have my name on them however the image of an accomplished entrepreneur in the making was an eerie replication of the image I had drawn in the seventh grade. This story gets a bit deeper. Alberta, my late Godmother, told me a story in 2014 of how, at the wee age of 4 I would go with her to the flea markets in Pine Bluff, Arkansas. At these flea markets, she stated that for .5 to .10 cents I would purchase broken old baby dolls and toys from vendors who had old toys. She explained that I would take them home, wash them, put parts on them that needed it and made them 'purty' again. Once these dolls were all ready to go, I would take them back to the flea market and sale them to other children and their parents for $1 or more. She stated that I would then take my few dollars of profit and go to the dollar store and buy new toys for myself or place the money in my piggy bank. She reminded me that I was an entrepreneur very young. She reminded me that it was in my nature to turn a profit!! More importanately it was in my nature to try to offer something back better than I had found it. I was a mini entrepreneur at the wee age of 4.

Somewhere in between the age of 4 and twelve (the seventh grade) I forgot my true nature and what I was comfortable with doing. I forgot that I had a natural knack for entrepreneurship. Years later I would again be tested with these two options: medical field or entrepreneurship. Although deep down I wanted to be a business owner, I still told my family that I was going to stay on the trajectory of being a doctor, a cardiologist to be exact. Yes reader yes, I have a calculus calculating, trigonometry, chemistry, advanced molecular biology formulating type of brain. It would have been quite easy for me to go to medical school and on to a life of medical practice.

While in my senior year in high school I took Advanced Placement courses, mostly high level math and sciences in preparation of going to college ready to dive in any pre-medical program. I spent my summer in between my junior and senior year as the only African American in a Pharmacy fellowship at the University of Colorado Medical Sciences. I was very serious about going down a medical path. I managed to gain acceptance into every college that I applied to with a full ride scholarship that would take care of my tuition for four years to any university of my choosing. What did I do? Two days before the college decisions were due, I chose to stay in Colorado and attend the University of Denver. DU is a private university that did not have a good science and pre-medical program. I skipped over Michigan State University, Duke, Hendrix College, and many others that were prime colleges with top rated pre-medical and medical programs. I chose to go to DU which was known for what? You guessed it... a robust and top rated business school called the Daniels College of Business. My intentions were very split but my actions were maneuvering towards my deeply desired destination of becoming an entrepreneur.

During my sophomore year in college I went from being an Honors Molecular Biology major to going undeclared and then later majoring in Business Management. I went on to receive my BSBA in Management. I started my company now called Phoenix Affect during my sophomore year as well. I won numerous awards from the university for my journey within entrepreneurship. I later went on to teach as a guest lecturer in that business school and as an Adjunct Faculty teaching my own mental health and wellness curriculum at the University of Denver's Colorado Women's College. The reconciliation for me is that my second business was called Phitnus. It was a health and wellness brand that centered on holistic health for women starting with emotional attunement. I reconciled my love for health and medicine by creating a line that made women feel great while also providing them with vitamins and a dance system amongst other things.

The lessons in the early part of my journey were invaluable. I learned to become one with what my true desires and intention were. I learned to listen to my core and follow through with the path that would be fulfilling for me versus one that would be pleasing to those around me. When you know, you know. Do not hesitate and do not take an absorbent amount of time to get on the path that you already know is the one for you. Anytime you have a thought that makes you feel good. Not the "ooh I saw something on TV that I desire that makes me feel good" or "ooh this food is so delicious it makes me feel good," but the "this moment warmed my heart and inspired me" type of feeling. Those moments let you know that you are on the right path. Those feeling are there to inform you that you are within the proper flow of energy. Those moments can also help you figure out what your true intentions are.

Do you have any images of your younger self? Any kid pictures of yourself? Most people do. I have three of them to be exact. As a child, our home caught fire and many of our images were lost. Through the years I was able to scavenge up three of them. I have one of myself at the age of 5. That picture means so much to me because it was before I ever collected pain and negative experiences from other human beings. It was when I was fearless and compassionate and at that point I hadn't experienced my "Me Too" experience. It took years to get back to that child. In honor of her I walk past her most days. I wink at her. I stop and ask her if she is proud of me. I ask her am I doing her purpose justice. I ask her do I make her happy and is she fulfilled living within me. I ask her did I become everything that she has wanted to become and am I on the right path.

If you have an image of yourself as I child I would like for you to do the same. Sit the image in a place where you can see it often. Meditate on it or simply do as I do. Look at it. Smile at it. Kiss it. Tell it that you love it. Connect with it. Ask questions that you need answers to and direct it to the child within you. Honor the clear, powerful, and innocent spirit that you were by connecting with it as often as you need to. The emotions that arise from this can be tremendous however it is very healing. Your inner child could step out and inform you of everything you need to know, need to change and how to love yourself better. Take note of how this exercise makes you feel.

CHAPTER 10

COMMITMENT

"Make a choice. Decide what it's going to be, who you're going to be, how you're going to do it. Just decide and then from that point the Universe is going to get out of your way. Its water and it wants to move around stuff."

- Will Smith, world renowned actor, motivational speaker, & musician.

TAKING THE TIME TO PINPOINT and live within your intentions is hard enough however the tough part is making the definitive choice to *be something*. In our informational sharing world many do not know what they want to be or who they are internally. Many are a reflection of what is shown to them on television. One can go back to earlier television with shows like The Brady Bunch or The Cosby Show which showed the dynamic of large households and families. One of the shows, The Brady Bunch, gave an example of a blended family that merged two sets of genders to coexist within their two worlds. Chaos between the sets of children, everyday comedic situations occurred, and the age gaps between the children created dynamics that were very realistic as it were portrayed on television. One thing that was not as readily spoken about was the commitment that was made between the two adults who decided that there was enough love between them to merge two homes and enough children to fill a basketball lineup. With the sitcom The Cosby Show you had an affluent family with two full time working parents and five children of their own. Throughout the seasons they would allow their adult children, other family member's children, their grandchildren, and extended family members to live with them as they saved money or decided their path in life. The Cosby's made a commitment to be a pillar of their family and a safe haven for those around them as they decided what their life's journey would entail. Now I know these are TV shows however they both are great examples of individuals and couples making commitments to be selfless.

Blended families and multi-generational households have become the norm in the United States as it has already been the norm around the world, at least people having multi-generational households. Interestingly enough a lot of this is going on within the millennial generation. About 13-50% of us ages 18-34 live at home with parents after going off to college (or not) and due to the unstable economics that are currently happening, many do not see a long term solution to live on their own. The younger millennials are at a higher percentage in the bunch for heading back to the nest. Whilst it is tough to find positions within certain industries, students go to college, go into debt and do not have a sufficient career position to pay off those debts. When one feels skeptical about the type of job they can procure or the amount of wages they can make, they become shifty about the educational decisions that they have made. This makes it that much harder to be definitive moving forward. If you are or have an adult child who is struggling with placement and where you want to be, first think about if what you are trying to do is what you have always wanted to do in the first place.

If you want something to open up or to manifest in your life, you have to make a firm decision about what you want. Oh goodness that is such a tough thing **Puts my hand on my forehead and faint into the pillow**. It is so tough, at least from my personal experience, to figure out what do I actually want. There is such a thing as having too many options. There are so many career paths, so many options for starting a business or a nonprofit, and so many talents to choose from. There is so much need in the world. I am a firm believer that you do not have to do one thing well as many believe. So many people, I am sure including yourself, have so many things that you are not just competent at but that you are great at! How dare anyone tell you to choose between which one of these to express. I would refrain from choosing between which talent or expression to focus on as you deal with the public and suggest that you choose and make a commitment to the talent(s) or expression(s) which lead you down the path towards your ultimate intention.

As you make a commitment towards your future and who you want to be in your future consider what you can let go... Yes you have let some things go. You have to release behaviors and even some skills that do not serve you. If you want to move clearly down a path towards your ultimate destination you have to keep yourself focused by removing the things that do not quite fit along that path. If you want to become a musician, learning how to frame images may not be a skill that you need to take on or continue to put energy into within your life.

Now let me be clear, this does not mean that you should not be practical and perform jobs or skills that could potentially fund your ultimate dreams. A person can work within a career that they do not like or that they do see as their end all be all *if and only if* it is being used to fund their true expression and dreams. I do not believe in having a job just to have one or to place oneself in a space of bondage if you do not have to. If you truly love what you do then keep on doing that and you can treat any business that you create as just an outlet for you. However do not get comfortable within a space that you know you do not want to be long term. Make a commitment that one day (and set a deadline) you will be fully out of the position and on to what will truly make you happy.

The word commitment scares so many people as they may associate it with finality. Nothing is final in our world, literally nothing. We as human beings are not even final. Transience and change are the only true things that are constant. We all have the right and the will to change our minds at any given point. We all have the right to reinvent ourselves or our lives, leave marriages/unions, walk away from situations that are not fitting to the spirit that we are evolving into, at any given moment. I say this as one who have broken a couple of commitments and who have been stamped firmly within other commitments. Even through the ups and downs of being a business owner, I wouldn't trade my years at Phoenix Affect for anything. I made a commitment to keep working at it and to keep on a path of making the business the best form of expression for me as I possibly could. There are going to be ebbs and flows within every situation however your commitment to it will determine how many phases of upward flows your experience. Are you ready to make a commitment to move towards your true desires and intentions?

CHAPTER 11

ACTIVATING DISCIPLINE

So how does one make such a life defining decisions as "What is my purpose?" or "What should I do next?" Discipline is how. I am not sure about you however I hated the idea of discipline for so long. I sort of still do to be honest. Goodness. The thought of doing things in order and with purpose everyday or nearly every day was daunting. With over a decade in business, doing what I wanted, traveling when I desired, spending and living how I preferred, became the normal for me. I didn't realize that I was also being incompetent in business, disappointing some clients, having lazy bouts, playing more than working and missing deadlines and opportunities.

It took certain things in my life to occur (mainly financial mishap) for me to realize that I needed to evolve and make better long-term decisions. I knew that it was time for me to shift gears and create a step by step guide for myself to stay centered and focused on my path. Below are seven incremental steps that can help instill discipline and complete milestones that matter.

1. Stay focused – In subsequent chapters you will learn about the various forms of distractions and how to increase your level of fo-

cus. First things first, have the intention to maintain focus. Start there. Do not begin anything without the intention of finishing it. In whatever way that is necessary, make singular focus your priority.

2. Prioritize task – Pick that one major project that you want to complete and start with the simplest task and those that you can knock out of the way fast. As you create that task list and knock those items out, it will be inspiring and uplifting to see the progression. Even if that progression is by a menial task ie "Purchase the domain for www.PhoenixAffectUniversity.com." Simple enough right? You can go to www.GoDaddy.com set aside $11.99 and purchase the domain. Task done. It took you five minutes however it is 10% of the task list. Awesome!

3. Get enough sleep! – What are your sleep patterns? Are you aware of them? Do you know if you get enough sleep on a daily basis or if you are surviving off of sleep deficit? This was my pattern: Wake up at 7am, get my son ready for school, drop him off, come home and sleep until 10or 11am, rise again and start working until 4pm, pick him up, come home, nap again for an hour, wake up and work until 2am. Repeat. Somewhere between the evening nap and 9pm I cooked diner, helped with homework, and slightly entertained an only child. If of course I wasn't somewhere at a board meeting, speaking or apart of some evening based event. How horrible is this?! I was never as efficient as I could be. I was never full of energy for more than a few hours. My body could not sustain the lack of sleep or sporadic sleep I was experiencing. To receive the benefits that sleep have to offer, we have to allow our body to fully immerse into deep rest. We have to set ourselves up for sleep success! Adequate sleep can create a very aware and high wired mind. It can produce a clear flow of energy that is able to pick

up on positive thoughts quicker. Sleep is important. You cannot dream if you do not sleep! If you need a little assistance in finding and creating your ideal sleep routine, visit <u>www.PhoenixJackson.com</u> and sign up to receive access to my free library that has a magical morning and evening routine creator. It will help you get your circadian rhythms on track and prepare you to be ready for the world as the world is ready for you.

4. Get your energy from good food – Our diet plays a significantly major role in maintaining a positive energy flow. I know that it is such a cliché however it is definitely true. You are what you eat. Everything we ingest becomes a part of our DNA and our cellular makeup. When we are sluggish in energy and lethargic we have to first examine how restful we are and second, we have to examine what we have ingested in the last 24 hours. Originally food was used to nourish the body and keep it healthy. Food has become a decadent thing that we savor and devour not taking into account the affects that this highly infused food can do to our body and our minds. Consider ways that you can alter your dietary intake to infuse more green foods and supplements. This will give you the extra boost that you need daily.

5. Do the small things – As it was mentioned before, while creating your to do list, knock off the small things first. It will indeed raise moral and keep your energy at a peak knowing that you are getting *something* done. If you are like some in which you have to have a clean environment in order to work efficiently, make sure your environment is prepared at night so that you can wake up and dive into the most important tasks your day has to offer. Start small and then elevate upwards.

6. Back track – Once you have completed your task, take some time to go back through and examine the importance of those steps be-

ing complete. Take the time to go back and follow up on those goals or task that have extra steps or have things that now need to be completed and were contingent upon the first step being finished. Reach out the people and things that require follow up, whether it is an email, a phone call, or an additional task. Look back but stay ahead of the curve.

7. Breathe and reward yourself – Look at you! Now that you have taken the time to outline what needs to be done, completed those things, you now can set yourself up for a little fun in the Sun (or the snow). I have a habit of creating blockages for myself to things that I love doing in hopes that I get the things done that I hate doing. I tell myself that I cannot travel to XYZ until I complete A-W. That's not happening. There are times when I pre-rewarded myself because my hard work creates a result faster than I expected and without being fully complete. However more than not, I stick to finishing what I set out to accomplish and then I give myself room to indulge. It is a great way to reward and honor yourself for all that you have done for... yourself.

A gateway to discovering your purpose is to complete things that you set out in front of yourself to complete. You will quickly realize the things that make you excited and those things that feel very draining. Those moments that drain you are informing you of what you do not want. They are giving you that uncomfortable pinch in your side letting you know that this particular thing does not work for you. Listen to those moments. Those feelings are here to teach you about what will work for you. The tasks or projects that truly excite you listen to those as well and create more of them. We all inherently know what we are meant to do; we just have to take the time to remember. Doing things that you dislike will remind you very quickly that you may not be on course to your desired destination.

SECTION 4

GET TO BUSINESS

Chapter 12

DISTRACTION. CATALYST. DETERRENT.

What does it mean to really move towards success? As we examine the ideas of success (especially in this modern age), it has everything to do with outer appearance and perception for most. One truth that many successful people come to realize is that accomplishment means nothing if a) you do not have someone to share it with and b) if you are not content with what you are doing and if you are not happy with where you are.

What does success truly mean to you? There is no wrong answer however what is not a good answer is that success doesn't mean anything to you or not having an answer at all. Many do not have an answer to the question and I personally blame this on the "noise" that we have around us at every waking hour. Geesh!

Being inundated with "noise" is the norm in our world. Noise falls under one of the following themes:

A distraction: Anything that distracts or takes you away from having consistency and drive towards a goal.

A catalyst: Something or someone inserted or removed from your life that changes the course of your journey.

A deterrent: Anything that can shift your emotional state at any given time.

Let's go into depth about these 3 forms of noise.

A DISTRACTION.

If something is not helping you grow, aiding in your intellectual expansion or adding positive attributes to your world then it is a distraction. The word distraction is defined as a thing that prevents someone from giving full attention to something or someone else. A distraction can be a person, a situation, an emotion, a device, etc. In today's world the largest and most prevalent distraction are our phones and other digital devices including tablets, TVs, and computers.

As it was mentioned before, if the Earth was only 24 hours old, humans would have arrived/evolved on it only 2 minutes ago... and in less than a decade or 1 second of our Earth day, social media and digital communication have absorbed the minds of the masses with the average person checking their phone and digital devices over 85 times per day! This number continues to rise. We have an addiction to distraction, the flow of information, and the idea of being connected to it all. The only major problem with this is that there is a major disconnect within this form of digital connection. As connected and wired in as we all are, many of us still long for a physical counterpart and face to face interaction. Humans were created and evolved this way. Just because we see all that is going on does not mean that we feel connected to it and furthermore we live in an age where *looking like you are doing something is more important than actually doing it.*

As a millennial, I blame this new way of being on us... we ushered in the age of falsified connection and experience. We are also the

Chapter 12 - Distraction. Catalyst. Deterrent.

generation that is struggling to find connection with people and things around us. We are trying to undo the damage that has been caused by our overzealous lack of inner growth due to our lack of true experience and connectivity. Much of our interactions on our devices are singular and do not require the presence of a counterpart. When people don't have much to do, instead of them sitting, reading or centering themselves, many look to the mini screens around them to provide some form of entertainment and comfort. Comfort now that is the magical word. To comfort in some way, shape, or form is the underlying effect of using distractions. We are seeking an escape out of our current reality and a break away for the mundane actions that we are performing. I understand it but if we truly want to get somewhere, we have to stop and slow down. Who knew slowing down could make you go faster? I did. We have to be ok with not being comforted.

Take a moment and imagine that you are at your local Motor Vehicle Department. You are sitting there, it is lit with fluorescent lights – you know those ones that are sort of dim and hang on the blue spectrum a bit so they make you sleepy when you look at them. Everyone looks a little worn and grungy, tired, and no one in there wants to be there, including the staff. "Number 264 come to window B," is said in the most monotone voice on the speaker system. Number 264 gets up from his seat, shuffles the papers in his hands and struts over to the window. Who knows how long he has been sitting there for his turn. As you look around you notice that most individuals are on their phones. They are either playing games, listening to music, watching something, reading something, talking to someone, or engaging on their social media. Their physical body is at the MVD however their mind is completely engaged elsewhere which means they ARE NOT IN THE PRESENT MOMENT. They are being completely distracted by a device that was made to distract them and to give them something to 'do'.

Our lives are a cyclical journey. Literally we are on a beautiful Earth that revolves in a circle around the Sun. Our Earth has a Moon that revolves around it and all along we are here going through every month within a routine way of being and every year within similar routines. We go to work every day (most of us), come home, interact or not with those with whom we live with, spend outrageous amounts of time on our phone or watching TV and then we do it all over again the next day. Many of us are always mentally in the MVD. We are always physically somewhere that we do not want to be so we check in to the digital motel to find comfort, solace and false connectivity. Many of us in the US in particular also indulge in many forms of substance intake to mask our perception of our world. Alcohol, cigarettes, marijuana, prescription drugs, mushrooms, heroin, sugar, food and more are all forms of substances that are used daily to distract and to check out of your daily reality. We have some of the highest rates of addiction in the world. With all of the material comforts and wealth that we have, we are still dissatisfied. It is time for us to go deeper. It is time to go within.

In order to find out how you want to express yourself to the world or what you will be good at, you have to take an assessment of what your distractions are so that you can remove. Removing distractions is a vital and an extremely important step in manifesting a life that is not one that you want to check in or out of.

What is your daily routine? What does it normally look like and what actions do you perform?

For example:

7:00am - Wake up and take a shower

8:30am - I leave home to head to the office

_____

_____

Chapter 12 - Distraction. Catalyst. Deterrent.

_____
_____
_____

What parts of your daily routine do you wish to change?

_____
_____
_____
_____

Why do you want to change these things? What do you not like about them?

_____
_____
_____
_____

Now to the juicy stuff, what do you do to distract yourself daily? (Be honest with yourself.)

_____
_____
_____
_____
_____

_____

_____

_____

_____

What do you feel you are getting from these distractions? Do these distractions change your world at all? Do these distractions make you tolerate your daily routine better? Do they make you happy?

_____

_____

_____

_____

_____

Let's say you woke up tomorrow morning and these distractions were nowhere to be found, what would you do to get through your days and nights?

_____

_____

_____

_____

_____

Let's take it a step further and say tomorrow you do take out half of your distractions and replace that lost time and energy with something evolving, something that will expand your mind, something that will expand you, what would you be doing?

Chapter 12 - Distraction. Catalyst. Deterrent.

_____
_____
_____
_____

Is there something that you really want in life? Is there something you want to have or an experience you want to achieve?

_____
_____
_____
_____
_____

The task item I am going to put before you is that you wake up tomorrow and remove just one of your distractions out of your life for one full week. During the week that you remove this distraction take some time to take note of how you feel. Sit down and take note of what goes through your mind. Write down if you are feeling physical, emotional or mental blockages that are trying to break through in light that you have been distracting yourself for so long and were not able to release those blockages. Write down how you feel about whatever you are feeling. Let's get rid of these distractions one at a time and see how your life tends to evolve. It is interesting but when you take one step towards balance in your life, our life tends to return the favor by making the next three steps easy to flow into. Life is a dance. Strut confidently and free your dependency on things that do not add to your existence.

A Catalyst.

There are times in our life where things occur when we least expect them to. We are strolling through life minding our own business and then BOOM something happens that completely shifts our way of life, the way we think or how we operate towards our external environment. I consider these moments to be catalyst. The word catalyst is defined as a substance that increases the rate of chemical reaction without itself undergoing any permanent chemical change. In other words, it is something or someone or an experience that happens within your life that alters your life or the course of your journey without changing itself in the process. It is something that happen to you.

When I was 7 years old I lived in Pine Bluff, Arkansas with my single mother and two other siblings. We went to school, played outside in front of our small brick two bedroom, one bathroom duplex home. We lived across the street from a beautiful inlet to the Pine Bluff River with a 50 ft cliff from the front door to the edge of the bank. We never got too close as we understood if you fell, that was it! It was a beautiful sight to see. I still long to live near water to this day partially because I saw the boats, the water and the sun shining off of the bank nearly every day. As a child I didn't understand the beauty of it nor understood how rare it is to live near water these days. With out of course it costing you a pretty penny or two. We were poor with many amenities that poor individuals in America can afford. However we didn't have as much access to money so my mother made decisions that would cost her her freedom with a prison term of a year and a half. Overnight, my siblings and I were swept up by our grandparents and moved to Little Rock, AR to wait for my father to come and gain custody of us. Within two weeks one of my siblings and I moved to Fort Campbell, Kentucky with my father and stepmother. My life would never be the same again. This is an example of a catalyst filled experience. As a child in one day I lost my mother, my maternal comfort, and the only world I ever knew. It was replaced with my father and those around him. This was a catalyst filled experience. So what changed for me that caused a shift in how I interacted with my world? I became on guard. After having understanding at a young age of my mother's plight, I still felt abandoned and this caused emotional detachment from anyone in fear of them one day being taken away from me. It took years for me to reconcile that experience and understand that no matter what happens to the people in my life (good or bad) I cannot limit my ability to open my heart and to experience fully. It took a while to fill the gaps that I had in my life starting with that first major catalyst.

Most individuals if not all have experience at least one major catalyst in their lifetime. Many Americans experience it when and if their parents go through a divorce. Are you missing a parent or did one of your parents leave early in your life? That was a catalyst. Did you experience a move to another city or state? Did you experience bullying or a challenging environment growing up? Did you go through something traumatic and/or unhealthy? Let's examine what your catalysts have been and how it may have changed your trajectory in life.

Please take a moment and think about all of the catalyst that you have experienced in life. List as many as you can and start up on a new piece of paper if you need to. I will leave space for three of them right here.

1. _____

_____

_____

_____

2. _____
_____
_____
_____
_____

3. _____
_____
_____
_____

Now let's analyze how you think these catalysts have affected you (whether positively or negatively.)

How did the first catalyst affect you:
_____
_____
_____
_____
_____

Did your life change for the better or worse (in your opinion)?
_____

Chapter 12 - Distraction. Catalyst. Deterrent.

_____
_____
_____
_____

How did the second catalyst affect you:

_____
_____
_____
_____

Did your life change for the better or worse (in your opinion)?

_____
_____
_____
_____

How did the third catalyst affect you:

_____
_____
_____
_____

Did your life change for the better or worse (in your opinion)?

_____

_____

_____

_____

_____

How about a power pause to pat yourself on the back. Truth is, despite what life has thrown at you, you have been indomitable and a formidable opponent. You are here now, conquering this next leg of your journey and preparing to soar. Many do not make it to the other side in one piece (metaphorically) after a catalyst has appeared in their life. If you haven't heard anyone say it before, I am telling you that I am extremely proud of you. Life is not easy and it is especially isn't easy for individuals who are meant to be powerful.

Do you think your life would be different had you not experienced those catalyst? How so?

_____

_____

_____

_____

_____

_____

_____

_____

_____

Do you think that you would be a different person with a different personality had you not of had those experiences? How so?

_____

_____

_____

_____

_____

Living in any form of regret makes one not fully present and appreciative of the present moment. Can you take time to accept what has happened? It is of my personal belief that EVERYTHING that happens to us is a manifestation of a pathway to become our highest self. It is almost like our brain and spirit is hardwired to create the idea circumstances in our lives to force us to become the best we can be for ourselves and for those around us. Again, if you put enough pressure on a coal, it will become a raw cut diamond. No pressure. No diamond. If you think that you would have had a different life and that you would have been a different person had certain circumstances not occurred in your life, what's stopping you from becoming that alternative individual and experiencing that alternative reality now?

What can you begin to do today to become the person that was not negatively impacted or affected by your past? (In this book there are so many ways in which I ask this same question. It is of the utmost importance that this question is answered continuously.)

_____

_____

_____

_____

A Deterrent.

Remember a few pages back you read about distractions? Well deterrents are somewhat of distractions because they are emotions or feelings that take you from one way of thinking and being to another without you even knowing. Deterrents keep you in a state of pause. A deterrent is defined as a thing that discourages or is intended to discourage someone from doing something. So many of our first deterrents happen by way of our parents or a guardian, who placed their limiting thoughts on to the child. Many times, as adults we create our own deterrent and excuses to slow ourselves down. Time is a deterrent, our full-time careers are deterrents, our family life and personal obligations are deterrents—if we allow them to be.

Many people plan to start businesses, they plan to reinvent themselves or they plan to take a leap into something new however they allow life to deter them from that course. It is important to get rid of every deterrent possible. We are already on a course of trying to survive, trying to live and trying to thrive. Living in a mode of discouragement is the last thing that anyone of us needs. If you are discouraged you are less likely to accomplish anything. To be in a state of discouragement leads to escalated fears, anger and depression. These emotional states encourage directionless behavior. Directionless behavior leads to a life lacking purpose and fulfillment.

What emotions do you feel when you feel stagnant or within a state of pause? What deterrents triggered these emotions?

_____
_____
_____
_____
_____

Do you think that there are some deterrents that can be removed from your life? Which ones?

_____
_____
_____
_____
_____

Can you start tomorrow with removing one of those? Which one and how do you propose to do that?

_____
_____
_____
_____
_____

Chapter 13

STRENGTH

Through trials and tribulations in life if we don't discover anything else, we discover where our strengths lie. If we are paying attention to the lessons of the season we also discover what our weaknesses are. In our culture we are told to focus on our weaknesses to make them better and to make them into strengths. However we are also told and also are aware of the fact that whatever we focus our energy on amplifies. Do you really want to focus on your weaknesses?

There are many aptitude test out there that reveals what your personality type is or literature that explains what your traits are expected to be if you are born during a certain part of the year or based on the numerology of your name, etc.. Many of these do carry levels of truth however this information can be limiting. If you read early on in life that you are only good in one area, you will focus your energy there and miss the mark of being a full self realized human being. Full realized human beings are all encompassing. They live in the 'AND'. Meaning they do not see life as Black and White, they notice the Grey and if they are lucky, they notice the full spectrum of the rainbow. They do not focus on their weaknesses... as a matter of fact they do not even acknowledge their weaknesses unless they become impediments. Do not get me wrong, it is smart to see your weaknesses however once you know that they are there, move on and place a spotlight on your strengths.

There are strength finding exams available online and the biggest strength finder is life itself. I took a test that displayed my top strengths being Communication, Strategizing, Intellection, Empathy, and Connectedness. This is easy, it basically says that I can speak well, I see my way through things and am able to guide others through and around things, I am smart, I feel what others feel and I can see the whole picture. Life had already taught me through experience that these were my strengths. Without taking an online examination or depending on a system to tell you more about who you are, let's look at your journey and extract out experiences where you have excelled.

Think about a situation in which you kicked ass! Maybe you conquered a fear, maybe you decided to do something spontaneously that turned out well; maybe you attract cool things and people (which would make you a great manifestor.) Write down the situation(s) here:

_____

_____

_____

_____

_____

_____

_____

_____

_____

_____

Pull out 3 strengths that you see shining in these situations. Here are some examples for you to consider:

1. I was the peace maker.
2. I am resilient.
3. I was able to find a great solution to a big problem.
4. _____
5. _____
6. _____

Everything we do is a form of expression. What type of service or product can you provide to the public that can somehow utilize those strengths? During my journey while realizing that I was an orator that could make my audience members feel various emotions from tears to laughter, I created a career and a speaker's bureau that gave me the room to express the strength of Communication and Empathy as often as I could. I figured, hey I can speak well, I should train others to do so, or I am great at Connectedness, how about open doors for others? Even better yet, I am intelligent, how about I teach what I know.

Consequently, if there are things that you are great at doing, how about find a way to make a living at it.

List 3 business ideas that you already have or list 3 based on the strengths that you listed: (If two strengths intersect that is fine.)

1. _____
2. _____
3. _____

Do any of these business ideas stand out to you as something you think will be really fulfilling? Do you think performing the task that the idea requires would be painstaking or will it make you feel elated? As you step into starting an enterprise do not be afraid to ask yourself these very real questions. Make sure that your intentions and desires are being met if you were to start this business. Does this business contribute to your final outcome or does it fit into the larger scheme of things that you picture for yourself? Again, do not be afraid to ask yourself these questions.

CHAPTER 14

STRATEGIC PLANNING

Enough of the deep diving. To be clear about the direction of the business one must have a plan! If you do not plan to succeed, you plan to fail. You need more than any old plan; you need a strategic business plan that maps out steps to your success. A strategic business plan can be used to help keep you on a doable timeline, help organize various portions of the business for yourself or others and to procure funding and clarity to donors.

Business plans are normally about 30 pages give or take 5 pages. They are compacted with enough information to be the guiding light for the business or organization. Below is a breakdown of the most important elements of the plan and what should be included therein. Every organization, business or hobby is different so some categories will need to be expounded upon as you create the plan. Let's consider what moving pieces are needed for a thorough plan. Keep in mind the business ideas you listed as you read through this list.

    A. Executive Summary – it is a 1-2 page summary of the entire business. It breaks down each section of the plan and shows the progression and succession of the business.

      a. Explanation of what the business is and what service or product it will provide.

      b. Feature the mission and vision.

      c. Feature a paragraph on each of the Operations, Management, Marketing, and Competition.

      d. Description of progression of the business.

      e. Description of what type of business or organization it is, for example a nonprofit, a S Corporation, an LLC.

      f. A written breakdown of the financial model and year to date profit/lost and balance sheet.

      g. Location and any scalable thoughts of expanding locations if there are any.

      h. Funding needed for business.

B. Company Description

      a. Are you providing a solution to a problem? Feature it here.

      b. Are you offering a product or series of products? Feature it here.

      c. Include your development to date and the legal structure of the business.

      d. History of the organization.

C. Industry Analysis

      a. Examine the industry in which your business or idea is surrounded within.

      b. Does your business fit into an industry or does it fit into multiple industries?

c. Do research and examine the strength or weaknesses in the industry and how your business can do something different as you grow.

d. Feature any economic, technological, regulatory and seasonal factors.

e. Are there any barriers of entry into your business? Cost, seasonal trends, etc.

D. Target Market

   a. Who do you want to buy your product or service?

   b. What area or demographics are you looking to launch your services or product?

   c. What is the market size and trends of the market and people you are marketing?

   d. What are the buying power and purchasing power of the people you are targeting?

E. The Competition

   a. Who else in the market both near and far also has the same services and products as you?

   b. How is the competition cornering the market?

   c. What are you going to do differently to stand out amongst the competition?

   d. Create a SWOT analysis to see how you can maximize your strengths and opportunities and minimize your weaknesses or threats.

F. Strategic Position and Risk Assessment
   a. What are you going to do different in positioning your company? Are you going to be high end, affordable, are you in the position to be the First Mover (the first person in your market to do what you do)?
   b. Market Risk- What will you do to minimize marketing mistakes to the public. Analyze any foreseeable mistakes.
   c. Competitive Risk- Once you enter the market in what way can your competition attack you or your product/service? Can they duplicate your processes easily? Do you need copyrighting or trademarking?
   d. Technology and Product Risk- Are your systems ready to go? If you launch a website that goes viral, can your server handle it?
   e. Executive Risk- If you have a partnership in the business, in what way is that business going to be affected if the partnership has any form of strain. Creating an exit strategy is ideal.

G. Plan of Action
   a. Layout to do list and task in three month increments for the course of a calendar year.

H. Marketing Plan
   a. Include visuals here with examples of your logo, tagline, business card design, flyers, website layout and/or mock ideas of what you like.
   b. Explanation of marketing vehicles and strategic partnerships.
   c. Social media engagement plan.
   d. Digital and print marketing strategy.

I. Operations and Management
   a. Include your role and any other roles that will be featured in the company. Include strengths.
   b. Where will the business operate and who all will be operating it?
   c. What are your personnel needs?
   d. For funding purposes, be sure to include resumes of key personnel and other background information that may be pertinent.
   e. What is the guiding corporate culture that you plan to create?
   f. Does your business/nonprofit require an advisory board or committees?

J. Technology
   a. Do you need any technology to operate your business?
   b. What hardware or software is required for your success? (Think Quickbooks, smart guides from other businesses, Adobe products, etc.)
   c. What type of website do you need? (Ecommerce, high database driven, something custom or portfolio based.)

K. Legal Review
   a. Include information about your operating agreement and articles of incorporation (you do not have to include official documents unless requested).
   b. What licenses or permits are needed for your business or industry?

c. Do you have a lawyer who is available for advice or legal representation? If so list them and their credentials.

d. Purchase business insurance if needed.

L. Community and Social Responsibility - Every business that my firm has worked with over the years must have this clause. Your business should aim to better society in one way or another. Think long term and think selflessly.

a. Include community outreach and community involvement.

b. Develop long term relationships with organizations that can benefit from your retained earnings and donations.

M. Development to Date

a. Milestones achieved to date.

b. 1 year, 3 year and 5 year goals for the business.

c. Strategy for achieving goals.

d. Expansion ideas and list risk associated with expanding if there are any.

e. Exit strategy, succession and contingency plan.

N. Financial Summary

a. Income Statement

b. Cash Flow

c. Balance Sheet

d. Break Even Analysis

e. Include any financial assumptions you may have about the quarterly growth associated with the business.

f. Include all charts and graphs necessary to visually explain your planned financial growth.

If your strategic business plan has all or most of these elements, it will be succinct and clear enough for you to use it as a guide to success. DO NOT make it a chore to create a plan. Take time as needed and chop it up in phases and use it as a time to manifest and think about how you want your business to truly operate. Use your imagination and think about what the perfect business looks like to you. This is different for everyone. Some love the idea of being a Solopreneur and some love the idea of creating a Transnational corporation employing thousands. Whatever your dream business is, use your plan as a way to manifest it! Put the plan in place and then refer to it weekly or monthly to see how it can be modified. Also use the plan to analyze how your business is progressing.

CHAPTER 15

BEGIN CREATING

MANY ASK WHY WERE WE created or brought to this planet to reside. It is one of my core beliefs that we were brought here to co-create and learn the art of manifesting in this physical three-dimensional reality. Furthermore, individuals who have a high capacity to create have a higher responsibility to create with and for the masses. When they are not creating their world reflects it. Those with high creative capabilities carry dense vibrations and thus have a deep responsibility (there goes that word again) to push society forward into a positive direction. The word positive means different things for everyone however I would categorize positive to include not harming the planet, not harming/killing other humans or any form of life and elevating the minds on the planet. The truth of the matter is we are all heading in the same direction whether we want to believe it or not.

If we kill our planet we kill ourselves. If we kill another, we kill ourselves. What is within me is in the whole and what is in the whole, is in each of us. The things that we hate the most are a reflection of the hate we carry in us, it isn't even about the things that we are directing our hate to and likewise the love that we carry within us is reflected outward in the things that we love the most. As you build your business make sure that it is something that you love or that you could grow to love. Your business is a form of your expression to the world. Make it count, make it not only make our lives easier but more meaningful and purposeful. Every spirit is responsible for where this world evolves into. Every spirit is responsible for the world.

During my freshman year of college, I went to see Dr. Maya Angelou speak. She was a bit frail and elderly in her older age however her spirit radiated as bright as the day she was born. She made a saddening statement of apology of the state that she was leaving the world and the state in which her generation had left the world. I felt sad empathizing with her in the moment. My emotions were where they were because I didn't understand then the truth of how each of us have a duty of collective impact. Where we leave this planet and where we leave the state of humans around us is very much on us. We must bear the weight of it whether we believe it or not. As an individual, Dr. Angelou did more than her fair share of elevating humanity. Her one spirit did more than a million other individuals combined. For this reason alone, I love and also forgive spirits like hers who came and left. If she hadn't been here, we would be even worse off. She did her purpose work while on this Earth. Will you?

As you evolve into being a person within business, observe your perceptions of yourself or of what you think you should be doing and being. There is no blueprint to your spirit and how it needs to express itself. You are unique, powerful and ever evolving. As a spirit who wants to interact on a merchant level on this planet make an agreement to consciously bring a level of positive interaction that people can feel as they interact with you within service or by consuming your product. Push forward the collective. We need your expression and your creations. We need you. You are who you choose to be, never forget this. Now create. Now build. Your community and the world is waiting.

You can purchase accessories to the book at

www.SpiritofBusinessBook.com